SCIENCE IN OUR WORLD

ELECTRICITY
and
MAGNETISM

Contributory Author
Brian Knapp, BSc, PhD
Art Director
Duncan McCrae, BSc
Special photography
Graham Servante
Special models
Tim Fulford, MA, Head of Design and Technology, Leighton Park School
Editorial consultants
Anna Grayson, Rita Owen
Science advisors
Clive Williams, Senior Engineer, Southern Electric plc
Jack Brettle, BSc, PhD, Chief Research Scientist, Pilkington plc
Production controller
Gillian Gatehouse
Print consultants
Landmark Production Consultants Ltd
Printed and bound in Hong Kong
Produced by EARTHSCAPE EDITIONS

First published in the United Kingdom in 1991
by Atlantic Europe Publishing Company Limited
86 Peppard Road, Sonning Common, Reading,
Berkshire, RG4 9RP, UK
Tel: (0734) 723751   Fax: (0734) 724488

Copyright © 1991
Atlantic Europe Publishing Company Limited

Reprinted in 1992

British Library Cataloguing in Publication Data
Knapp, Brian
  Electricity and Magnetism
  1. Electricity and Magnetism– For children
  I. Title   II. Series
  537
        ISBN 1-869860-70-5

All rights reserved. No part of this publication may be reproduced, stored in a retrieval system, or transmitted in any form or by any means otherwise, without prior permission in writing of the publisher, nor be otherwise circulated in any form of binding or cover other than that in which it is published and without a similar condition including this condition being imposed on the subsequent purchaser.

In this book you will find some words that have been shown in **bold** type. There is a full explanation of each of these words on pages 46 and 47.

On many pages you will find experiments that you might like to try for yourself. They have been put in a coloured box like this.

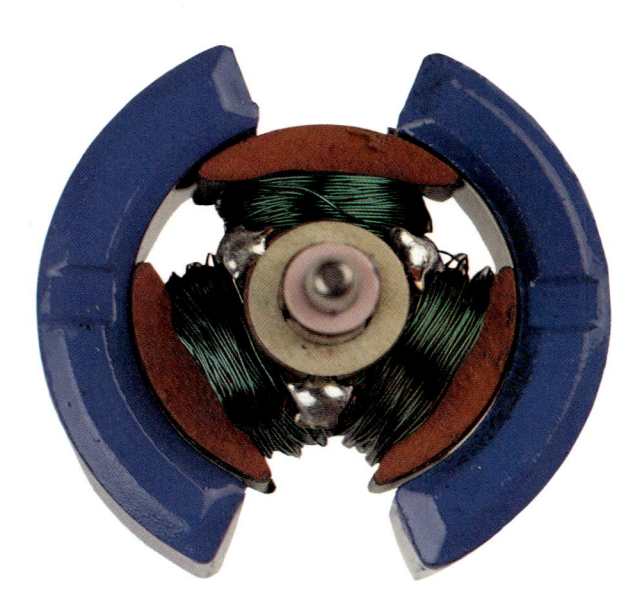

Acknowledgements
The publishers would like to thank the following:
Andrew Burnett, Irene Knapp, Leighton Park School, Micklands County Primary School, Redlands County Primary School and Southern Electric plc.

Picture credits
t=top b= bottom l=left r=right

All photographs from the Earthscape Editions photographic library except the following:
Ann Ronan Picture Library 4, 11, 38;
ZEFA 5, 11, 44/45, 45.

Contents

Introduction	Page 4
What is electricity?	6
Look for a charge	8
Electricity in nature	10
Conductors and insulators	12
Home supply	14
Heat, light or safety?	16
All in a line	18
Getting plugged in	20
Watt's it cost?	22
Carrying electricity about	24
Electrifying coats	26
What is magnetism?	28
Follow the field	30
Magnets on demand	32
Magnets with a memory	34
Electric motor	36
Tell the world	38
The speaking magnet	40
Making electricity	42
Magnets in space	44
New words	46
Index	48

Introduction

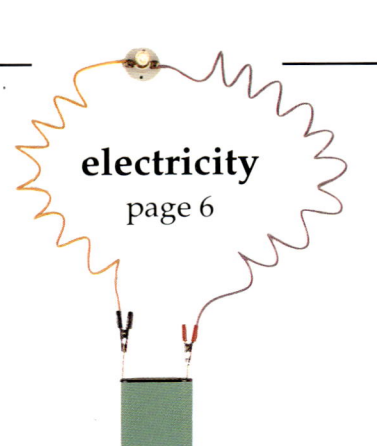

electricity
page 6

compass
page 30

nature
page 10

heating
page 16

telegraph
page 38

Look around you. You live in a world that is worked by electricity. You cannot see it, feel it, hear it or smell it, but as if by magic, it is always there when you want it.

By turning night into day electricity has changed the way we live. No longer do we have to haul coal, pump water, light candles, or shiver in our beds. Instead we simply have to flick a switch and we get unlimited power to play music, work the television, cook the food and wash our clothes. Through electricity we can speak on the telephone and store information on a computer.

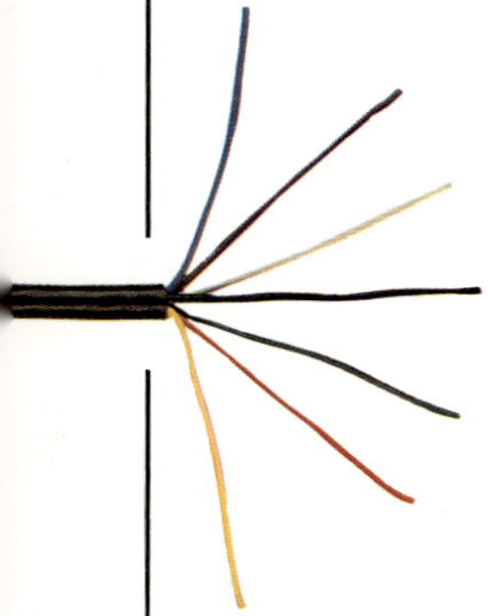

cables
page 12

static
page 8

home supply
page 14

connections
page 20

electromagnets
page 32

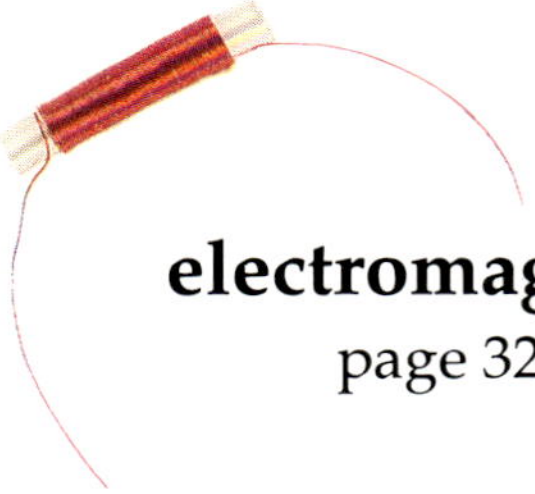

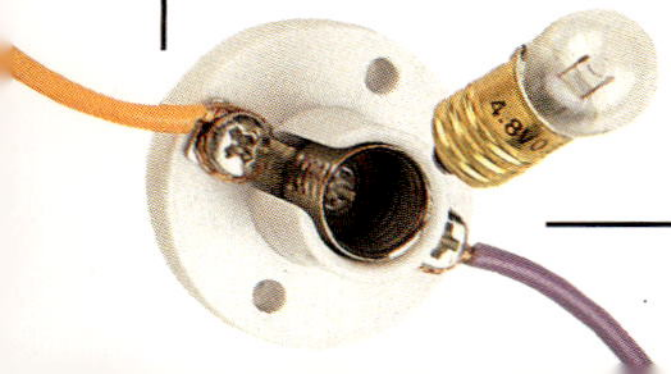

dynamo
page 42

costs
page 22

plating
page 26

party lights
page 18

Electricity can be carried around, to work toothbrushes and cassette players, torches and automobiles and even to power satellites as they spin high above the Earth.

You also live in a world of magnetism. Magnetism will sort rubbish, hold doors closed and work compasses; it helps migrating birds to fly round the world and, above all, it makes electricity. In fact, electricity and magnetism cannot be separated as we shall see later in this book.

Find out about electricity and magnetism in any way you choose. Just turn to a page and begin your discoveries.

motor
page 36

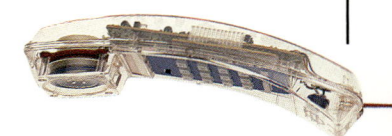

telephone
page 40

tapes
page 34

sky lights
page 44

batteries
page 24

magnetism
page 28

What is electricity?

Mains electricity can kill. This is why all the interesting things you will find to do in this book use batteries rather than the mains. **Never, never touch the mains either at switches, sockets or by opening anything that is connected to the mains.**

Electricity cables are a very common sight. In the cables flows the **energy** to power many of the things we use. But because we cannot see electricity moving it can be very difficult to understand. Here are some simple ways of thinking about how it works.

Show how electricity works

Electricity can flow along a metal wire or cable for much the same reasons that water flows in a pipe. The flow is controlled by the *pressure* forcing the electricity through the wire and the *thickness* of the wire.

You can see how electricity moves by using a watering can. Fill the can with water and stand it in the ground. No water will flow.

Start to tip the can so the spray end is lower than the water in the can. The water will now spill out of the spray head. This is because the water in the can is pressing the water out of the spray head.

In electricity the 'pressure' is called the *voltage* and the flow of electricity is called the *current*. The small holes in the spray head stop the water from coming out too quickly. It holds back, or resists, the flow of water. The smaller the holes, the less the water can spray out. Most electrical **appliances** hold back the current as they work. They act as *resistors*.

A torch bulb, the resistor, fitted in a holder and connected to the battery with clips and wires

This is a cable covered with orange plastic

A cable covered with purple plastic

How electricity moves
In this picture a battery provides the source of electrical pressure (the voltage) and an electric current flows from the black tab (negative) on the battery along the orange wire, through the bulb (the resistor that gets so hot it produces light), along the purple wire and back to the red tab (positive) on the battery.

If you added another battery you would increase the voltage (the electrical pressure) and the bulb would shine more brightly. It is the same effect as tipping the watering can more steeply.

Ask a grown-up to help you to make this **circuit** and prove that it works.

The black clip is fixed to the negative (–) tab

The red clip is fixed to the positive (+) tab

A torch battery, the source of electrical pressure

There are many experiments you can do with a simple circuit like the one shown here. It uses wires, batteries, bulbs and clips from a bicycle accessory shop.

Each experiment in this book uses the same basic set-up. To make sure your circuits always work, *follow the wiring exactly*.

7

Look for a charge

Electrical pressure (voltage) can build up on the surfaces of some objects. This is called an electric **charge**. Because it does not flow, this form of electricity is called **static**.

Sometimes so much static electric charge builds up that it jumps through the air and causes a spark. At other times we can feel it is there because it makes our hair tingle.

Hang balloons
One way of hanging up balloons for a party is simply to rub them hard against your jumper. Put them against the wall or ceiling and they will stay there, stuck by the invisible force of electricity.

Now tie two balloons together with pieces of cotton. Rub each in turn and then hold the cotton. The balloons will try to bob away from each other because they have the same positive charge.

Hair-raising experience

A special machine – called a Van de Graaff generator – produces an electric charge in the same way as rubbing a balloon on your jumper.

The static electricity builds up on a large metal ball. When people touch the ball their hair stands on end because each strand of hair has the same positive charge. The result can be quite startling!

Finding electricity

If you put your *finger* close to the screen of a television you will often hear a faint crackle. This is the sound of tiny sparks jumping between the screen and your finger.

If you put your *arm* near the screen you will feel the hairs begin to stand on end as if by magic. This is also due to the electric charge.

Making electricity

You can make electricity by rubbing a plastic comb vigorously on a woollen jumper or a silk cloth. If you bring your arm next to the comb you should be able to make the hairs stand on end. It gives a really creepy feeling.

If you have a graphite puffer (the sort used to lubricate locks) then you can scatter some on a sheet of paper and bring the comb towards it. See what happens.

Electricity in nature

Electricity is a vital part of the natural world. When you touch this page, for example, the pressure on your finger tip sends an instant signal along your nerves to your brain. The brain then sends electrical signals to the muscles to tell them how to react.

Most natural electrical charges are very small. Large charges can overload our systems and kill us. However, there are some very large charges in the world: the largest can even make sparks fly through the air.

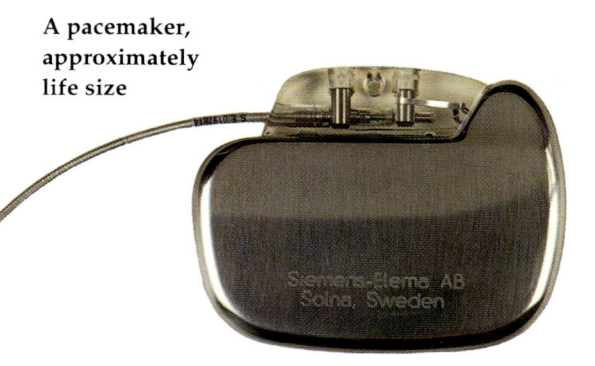

Staying alive
A heart constantly receives electrical signals or 'shocks' that make it twitch, or beat.

The heart has its own chemical battery that sends regular shocks to its muscles to keep it pumping. Some people get unreliable signals from this system. To make sure the heart never stops beating doctors insert an artificial 'heart kicker'. It is called a pacemaker.

The wire (called an electrode) from the pacemaker is lead through arteries to the heart. When the pacemaker senses that the heart is not working properly it sends tiny regular shocks to the heart to keep it beating.

A pacemaker, approximately life size

This is the pacemaker that is placed just under a chest muscle

This end is placed inside the heart. The small barbs make sure it stays in place

This cable is fed along the blood vessels that lead to the heart

Thunder and lightning

Lightning is a gigantic spark that goes from one part a cloud to another or between the cloud and the ground.

A *negative* charge builds up in a storm cloud because the air inside is tumbling over and over very quickly.

As the cloud grows the charge inside gets larger and larger. Eventually it is large enough to spark through the air to the *positive* charge on the ground. This is lightning.

Rod to catch the lightning

Wire to carry the charge safely to the ground

(For more information on thunder and lightning see *Science in our World, Volume 1, Weather*)

Lightning conductors

At the end of the eighteenth century umbrellas were fitted with metal rods so that if lightning stuck the umbrella it would be safely channelled away from the person holding it. Today lightning conductors are used on all tall buildings, but the chances of people being struck by lightning are small.

Conductors and insulators

Electricity can only travel through certain substances. These are called conductors. The wires that carry electricity are examples of materials called conductors.

All other materials do not let electricity pass through them. They are insulators.

Insulators
Some materials are better insulators than others. Air is a good insulator, but it is not always safe or convenient to rely on air. In cables, for example, conducting wires are very close together. In these situations insulators such as plastic are used.

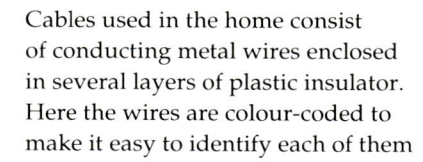

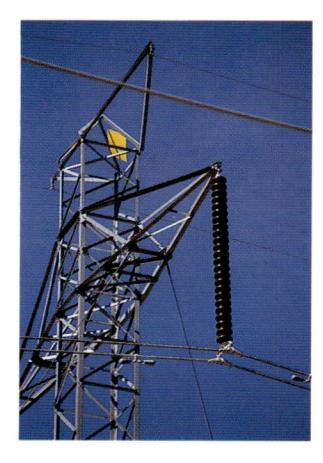

Cables used in the home consist of conducting metal wires enclosed in several layers of plastic insulator. Here the wires are colour-coded to make it easy to identify each of them

An electricity pylon

This insulator is used to separate the cables from the metal of the pylon. It is made of a material called a ceramic. It is similar to the china used in tableware

This is a conducting cable that carries electricity between pylons. It is made of a metal called aluminium. Notice how it consists of many wires twisted together

Air is used as the insulator for this cable. As it hangs from a pylon high above the ground it does not need a plastic coat

Bulb

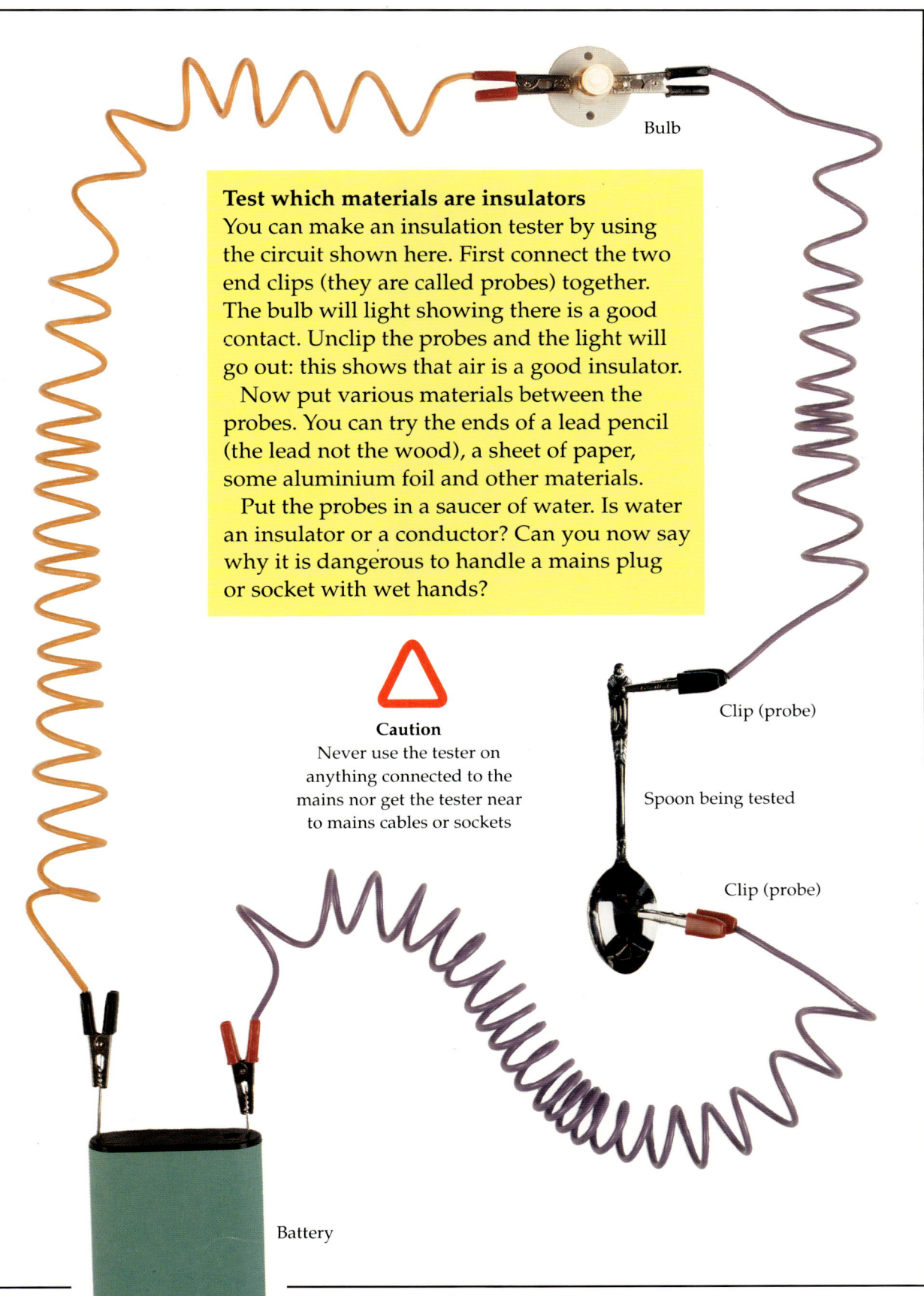

Test which materials are insulators

You can make an insulation tester by using the circuit shown here. First connect the two end clips (they are called probes) together. The bulb will light showing there is a good contact. Unclip the probes and the light will go out: this shows that air is a good insulator.

Now put various materials between the probes. You can try the ends of a lead pencil (the lead not the wood), a sheet of paper, some aluminium foil and other materials.

Put the probes in a saucer of water. Is water an insulator or a conductor? Can you now say why it is dangerous to handle a mains plug or socket with wet hands?

Caution
Never use the tester on anything connected to the mains nor get the tester near to mains cables or sockets

Clip (probe)

Spoon being tested

Clip (probe)

Battery

Home supply

The electricity that gets to your home has probably been produced a long way away. So how does it get to where it is needed?

Buried power cables are made from solid metal rods. This means that they are not very flexible and they can be hard to move around

Trunk cables
The cables that run from the electricity power stations carry very large amounts of **power**. They are trunk cables. The one shown here is as thick as your arm.

The outer red sleeve is plastic. It keeps moisture from the cable. Inside this is a metal tube to protect the wires from accidental damage.

Even the three wires inside the cable that carry the electricity are thicker than your thumb.

Flexible homes
Home cables also need to be flexible so that appliances can be moved about easily. Home cables are made flexible by using many strands of wire twisted together and protected with plastic coatings.

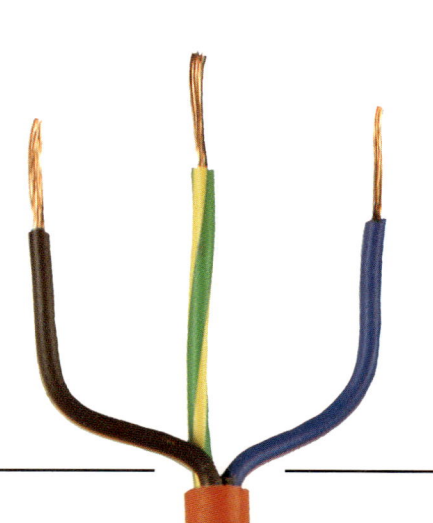

Hanging around
In this picture you can see cables connected to each house in a street from an overhead supply. Cables for each building are joined to the main supply at each pylon.

Wherever possible wires are buried underground because it is safer and more pleasant. However, burying cables is expensive and can only be justified in a built-up area. Electricity is carried on pylons in the countryside except near beauty spots.

Cables below your street
Trunk cables bring electricity to each district. They feed many smaller cables that run below each street.

Your home electricity supply is connected to one of these street cables. Ask a grown-up to show you where it is. It will be in the same place as the meter that measures how much electricity you use.

Heat, light or safety?

Most wires are made thick enough to allow the electricity to flow without getting warm, but special devices rely on hot wires to provide lighting, heating and even a safety switch.

Red hot
If a lot of electricity goes through a cable, the cable may heat up. This can be dangerous, but sometimes it is done for a purpose.
Inside a cooking element there is an insulated wire that is designed to get hot. The hot wire is used to cook food.

The heating wire is safely enclosed inside the metal tube. When the wire heats up, the heat is conducted through the insulation to the tube

White hot
If a lot of electricity flows through a thin wire, called a **filament**, it will first glow deep orange, then it will become yellow, then it will glow white. You can see this if you have a light bulb that is worked by a **dimmer**. The dimmer controls the amount of electricity passing through the bulb.

Fused

If an appliance goes wrong it may try to draw more electricity than is safe. If nothing is done the appliance may catch fire. To stop this happening, a special switch, called a fuse, is used.

A fuse is a thin piece of wire, rather like the filament in a bulb. If too much electricity flows in the wire, the fuse gets hot and melts safely inside its holder. By melting, the fuse breaks the circuit and switches the electricity off.

Every fuse has a value designed for a purpose. The number on the side of the fuse tells you how much electricity the fuse will carry before melting. It is not safe to put a big numbered fuse in a plug with a thin cable or the cable may melt before the fuse.

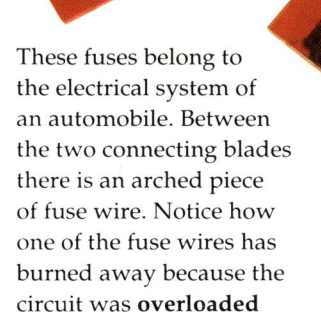

These fuses belong to the electrical system of an automobile. Between the two connecting blades there is an arched piece of fuse wire. Notice how one of the fuse wires has burned away because the circuit was **overloaded**

Caution
Never touch hot objects that are glowing red, orange or white. They can cause burns

17

All in a line

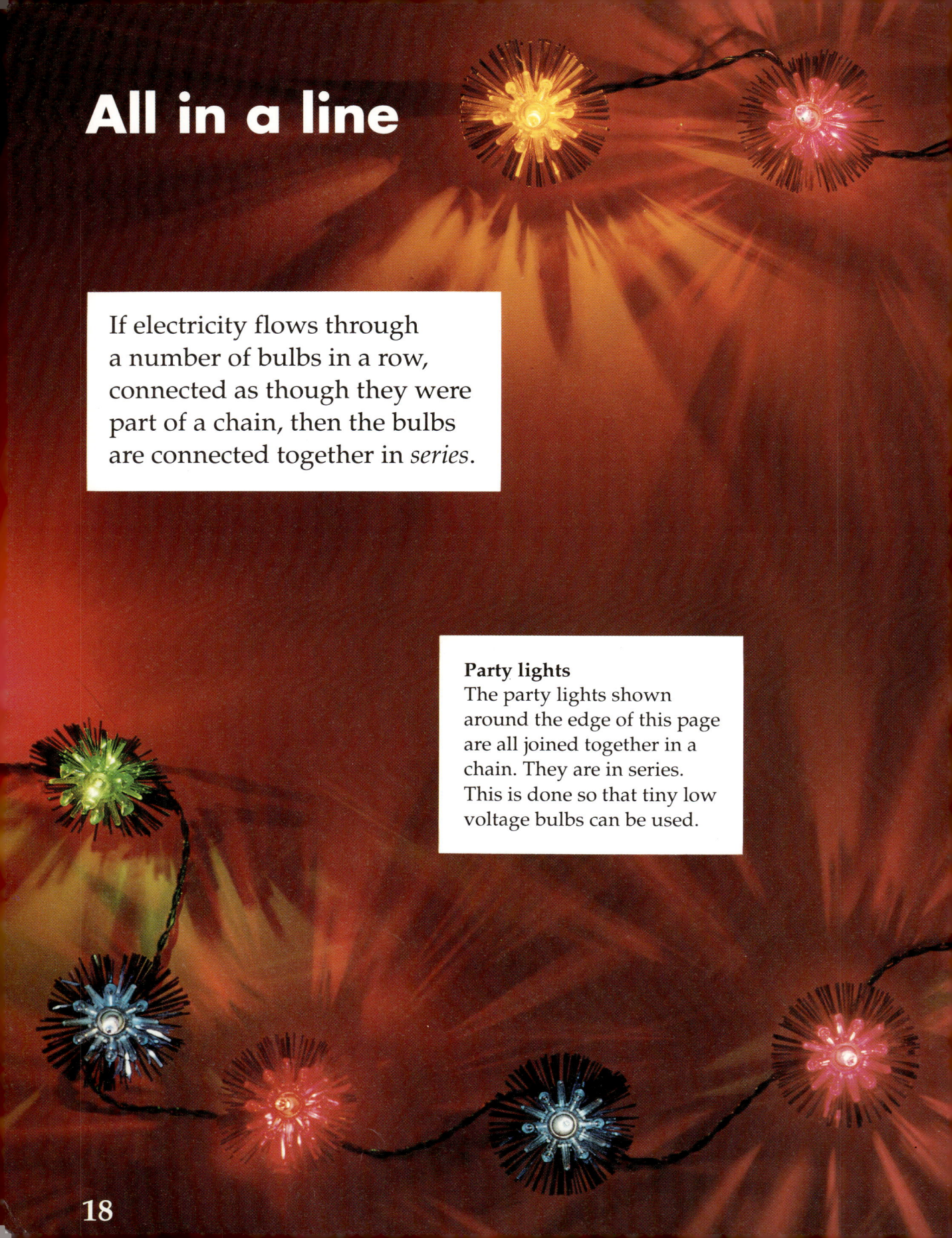

If electricity flows through a number of bulbs in a row, connected as though they were part of a chain, then the bulbs are connected together in *series*.

Party lights
The party lights shown around the edge of this page are all joined together in a chain. They are in series. This is done so that tiny low voltage bulbs can be used.

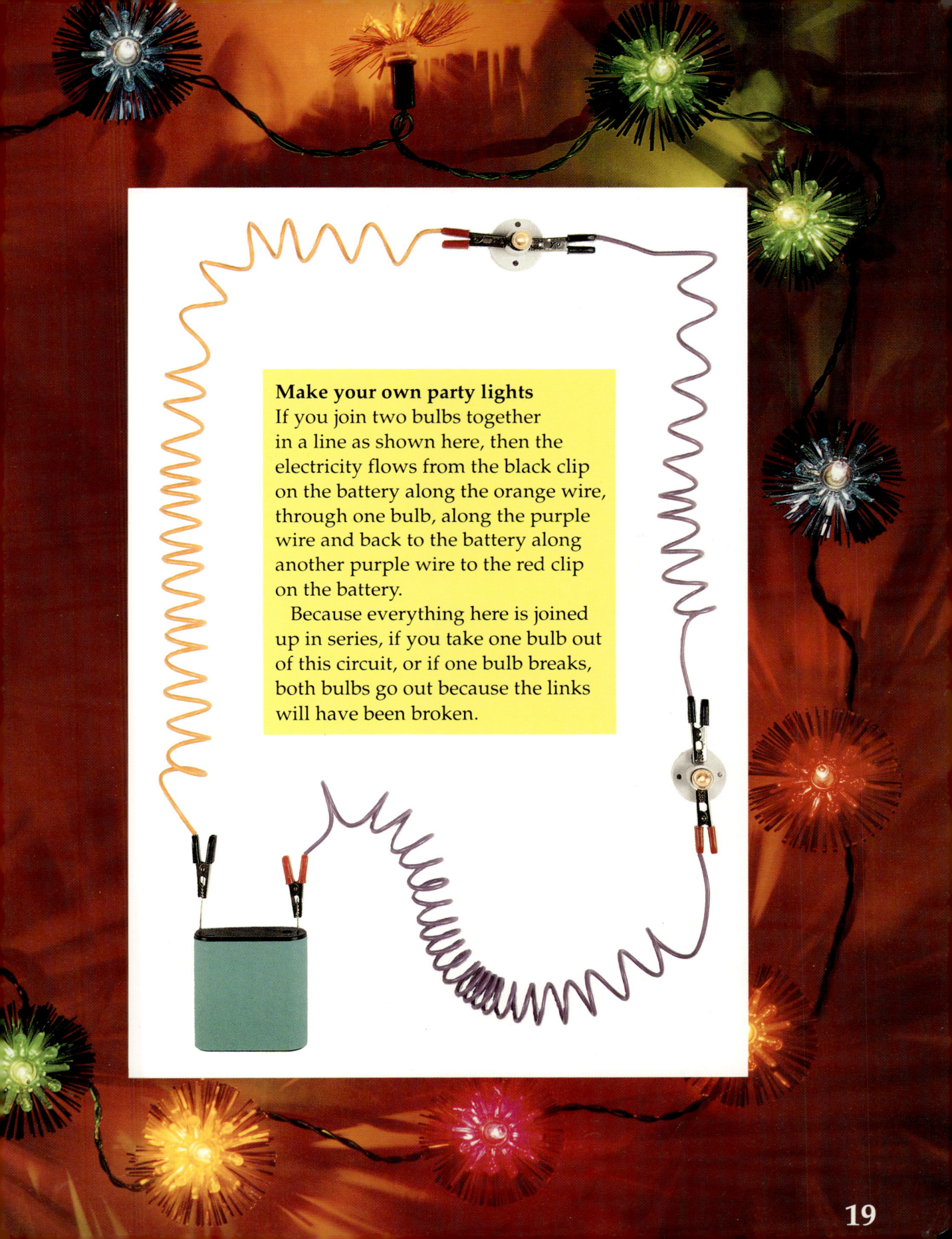

Make your own party lights
If you join two bulbs together in a line as shown here, then the electricity flows from the black clip on the battery along the orange wire, through one bulb, along the purple wire and back to the battery along another purple wire to the red clip on the battery.

Because everything here is joined up in series, if you take one bulb out of this circuit, or if one bulb breaks, both bulbs go out because the links will have been broken.

Getting plugged in

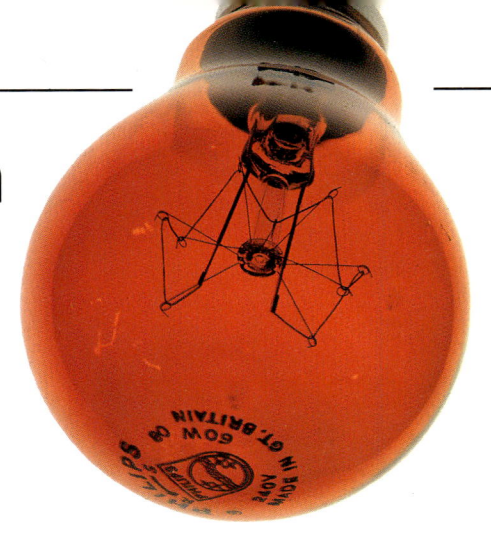

Have you noticed how any mains plug will fit into any mains socket? This means that, wherever you are, you can find a socket to plug into.

To make this possible people have had to design a way of making power available at every plug everywhere – so we can use it whenever we want. This is done by wiring in parallel.

The details of the mains bulb are on the glass. In this example they are on the crown of the bulb

Make it match in parallel
When you use bulbs in parallel they must be carefully matched. Often the plugs and sockets are designed to prevent mistakes. Bulbs designed for use with batteries are small and fit in special holders.

The mains is always 240V or 110V. Only mains equipment with the proper plugs can be used on the mains.

Home connection
If you look around your home you will find mains sockets in most rooms. These are connected together in parallel using cables in the walls and beneath the floor.

Sockets are a convenient way of getting the electrical supply to where it is needed. Each appliance can have the same plug and it can be connected up in any room we choose.

The voltage (V) is stamped here

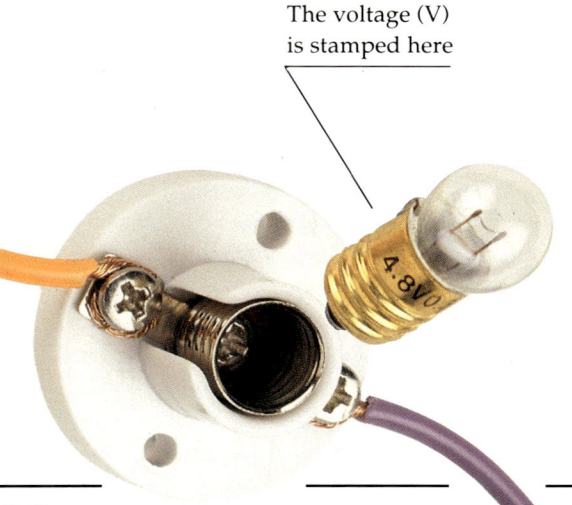

Plug-in bulbs have both contacts at the end

20

Wired in parallel

Try joining two bulbs to the battery in the way shown here. This is called a **parallel** circuit because each pair of wires goes to the battery and each bulb is connected directly to the battery.

When you have got the circuit connected and the bulbs are alight, unscrew one of the bulbs. Do you notice any difference in the brightness of the remaining bulb?

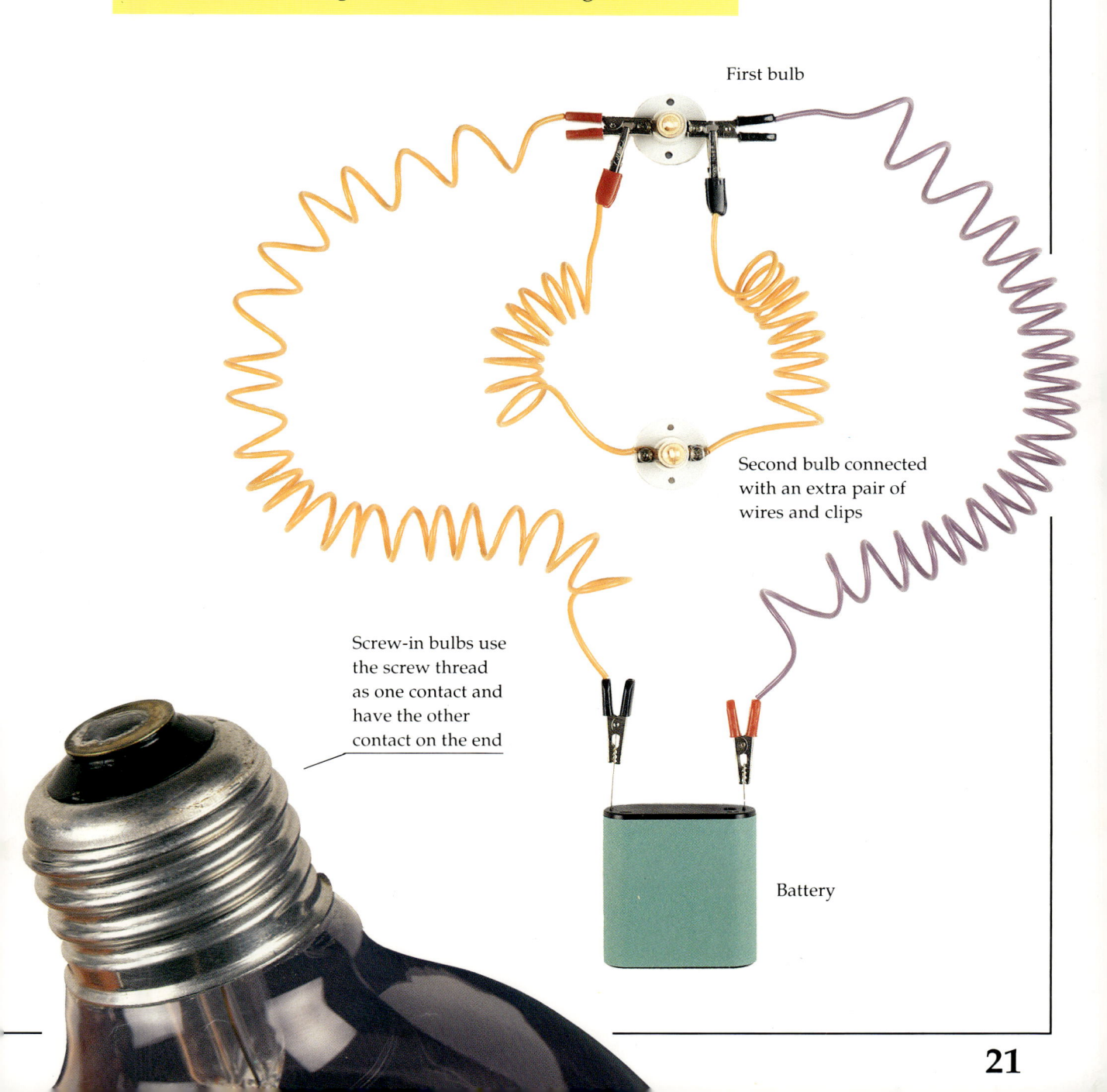

First bulb

Second bulb connected with an extra pair of wires and clips

Screw-in bulbs use the screw thread as one contact and have the other contact on the end

Battery

21

Watt's it cost?

All the electricity you use costs money. It makes sense to use it wisely and to know which things cost more to run than others. Here's how to find out how much electricity you use at home.

Watt's its value?
People measure the amount of electric energy in units called **Watts** (or W).

The amount of energy used is often marked on the equipment. If you look at a light bulb for example, you will find the value stamped on the top of the glass bulb.

Not all bulbs give out the same amount of light for the same amount of electricity. Light bulbs like the one above have a filament in them that gets very hot when it lights up. The heat is wasted energy.

New compact tubes like the one on the left are called fluorescent tubes. They run cool and waste very little energy. A 25W tube gives out as much light as a 100W bulb. This means that you can get four times as much light for the same money.

In the home
The amount of electricity you use depends on how much energy is needed. An electric kettle uses a lot of energy to boil water quickly. A typical kettle might use 20 times as much energy as a 100W light bulb.

A stove also uses a lot of energy to heat the element and cook the food. Each element may use about ten times as much electricity as a 100W light bulb. A stove is often responsible for a large part of a home electricity bill.

Big spenders

One of the most brightly lit places in the world is the city of Las Vegas. Thousands of light bulbs are used on the main street to give this dazzling display. But it uses up an enormous amount of energy.

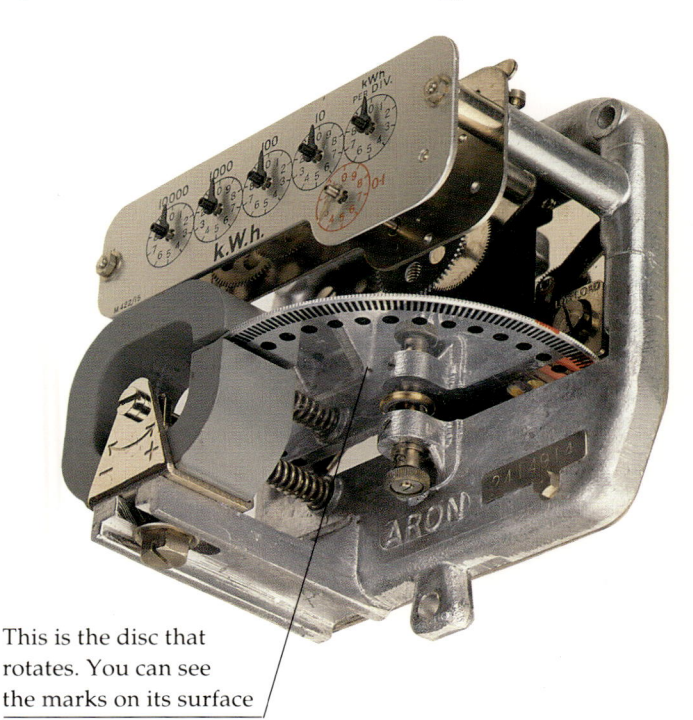

This is the disc that rotates. You can see the marks on its surface

Metered

The amount of electricity you use at home will be recorded by a meter. Ask a grown-up to show you where the meter is kept.

There will be a big disc in the meter. The faster the disc spins, the more electricity is being used. Make a record of the amount of electricity you use in your home during the day. Every hour look at the disc and find out how fast it is spinning. There are little marks on the edge of the disc. Count how many pass you in, say five seconds.

Make a chart of how fast the disc spins. Now try to find out what everyone was doing at each of the times. This way you can see which are the times when lots of electricity is used and what it is used for.

Carrying electricity about

Using mains electricity has one problem: you have to be close to a socket. This is not very convenient and a more portable form of electricity is often needed. This is why batteries or **solar** panels are used.

Solar cell

Electricity from light
You may already have a solar-powered watch or calculator. These are powered by a tiny wafer of material that makes electricity when light falls on it. It is called a solar cell. Light cells are a clean source of portable electricity.

Make your own battery
A battery is made of two different metals and a conducting liquid or paste. There are many natural liquids that are safe to use. One of them is the citric acid in a lemon (the acid gives the lemon its 'sharp' taste).

To make a lemon battery you will need a small strip of zinc and copper, (from a shop that sells building materials). Squash the lemon to release the juice. Use a knife to make slits in the lemon. Push the zinc and copper strips into the lemon and hold them to your tongue. The tingling feeling is electricity flowing in the lemon battery.

This is a self charging street light. In the day the solar panel makes electricity that charges a battery. At night the battery is used to power the street light

This Indian stamp shows a solar street light. Do you know of other stamps that show new forms of portable electricity?

A dry battery

A torch battery uses two materials such as carbon and zinc, plus a thick paste of special chemicals. They act in the same way as the lemon juice battery, but last longer and give more power. The case of this battery is made of zinc and it also makes the (−) negative connection. The carbon rod makes the (+) positive connection.

Many batteries run down when their chemicals wear out, although some batteries are made of materials that can be recharged.

Ordinary batteries also use about 50 times as much electricity to make as they supply. This means that, although they are convenient, they are not a good way of making electricity.

The chemicals used to make batteries are also harmful to the environment if they are not disposed of carefully.

Positive terminal

Carbon rod

Zinc outer case

Negative terminal

Chemical paste

Electrifying coats

Coating objects with a fine layer of metal is called electroplating. Many things are electroplated: from the layer that protects cars against rust, to the silver on knives, forks and spoons, and the metal coating on some plastics. These metal coatings will also conduct electricity, so they are often used in making computer and other circuits.

Caution
Do be careful with chemicals. Wash up afterwards and don't let any chemical get anywhere near your mouth

The principle of plating

This experiment shows the principle of electroplating. It uses a chemical called copper sulphate, a key and a copper wire.

When the electricity flows the copper is transferred from the bared end of the wire to the surface of the key. The key becomes plated in copper within seconds.

You might ask a grown up to demonstrate this experiment using a teaspoon of copper sulphate in a glass of water.

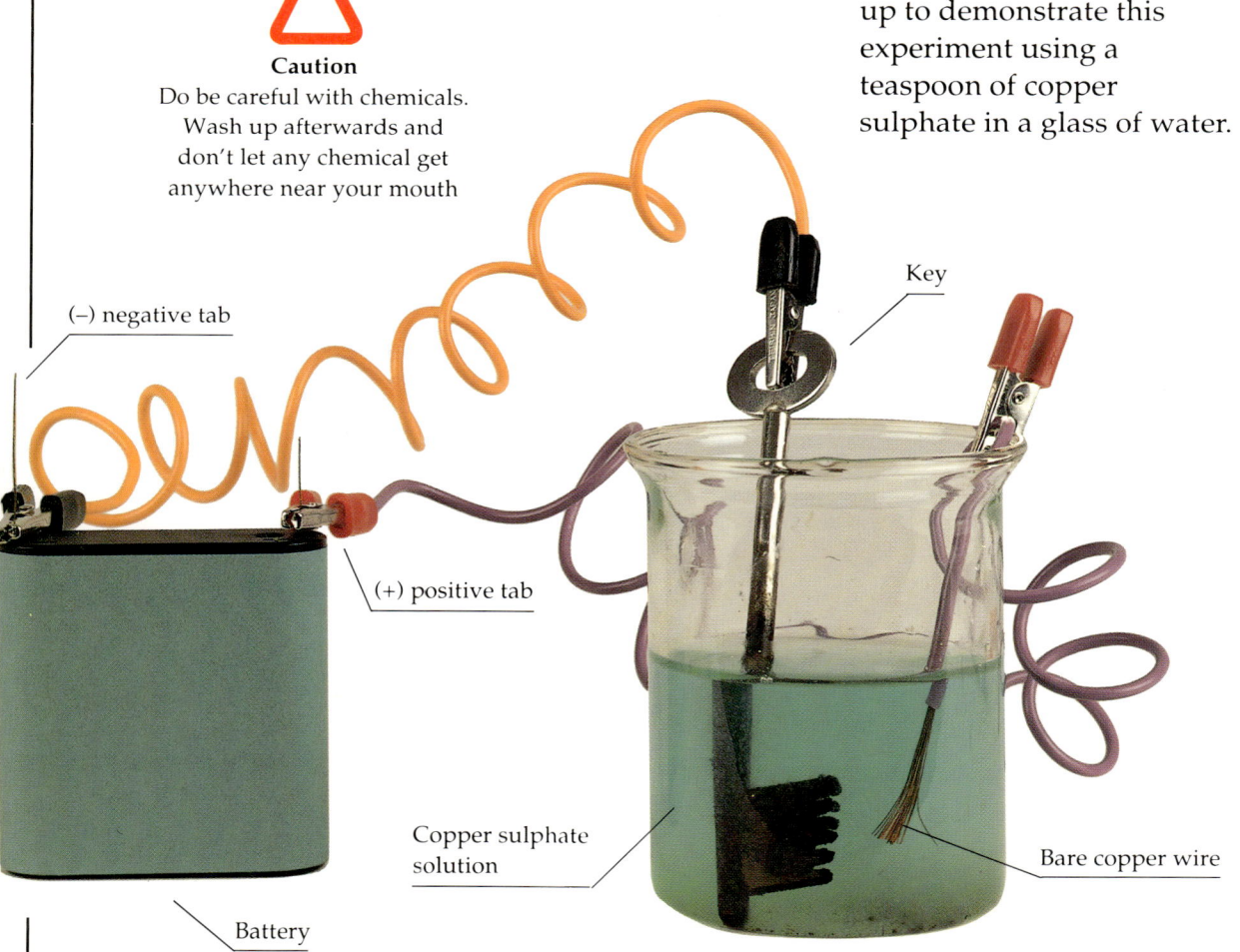

This is an orchid that has been plated with gold. A live orchid is shown in the small picture. Plated orchids make beautiful ornaments. The brooch comes from Thailand

Electroplating is very useful for coating complicated objects evenly. This tap is made of inexpensive brass with a surface coating of shiny, but expensive, chrome. This gives the hard wearing properties of chrome at a low cost

Solid silver items are very costly and they are soft. Silver plating covers a strong steel drinking goblet with a coat of silver to give it good looks

What is magnetism?

Magnets show us that there is a special force in the world called magnetism.

As with electricity, we cannot see or feel magnetism. But its effects are all around.

Magnets are easy to make and they have many uses.

What is a magnet?
A magnet is a material that attracts or repels other materials. A material becomes a magnet when all the tiny particles inside it become lined up in the same way.

A magnet has two places where the force is very strong. They are called **poles**. Every magnet, whatever its shape, has a north pole and a south pole.

Think of the poles as you think of electricity. Like repels and opposites attract. A north pole of one magnet will attract a south pole of another magnet, but it will push a north pole away.

All shapes and sizes
Magnets are often strips of iron or steel. Magnets can come in many strengths and in many shapes. Two common shapes are a straight bar and a horse-shoe.

You can find out how strong a magnet is by holding an iron nail in one hand and a magnet in the other. Bring them together until you feel the magnet pulling the nail. Another way is to see how many nails each magnet will pull out of a box.

Try different magnets to see how the strength varies.

The secret fastener
Magnets are used to hold doors closed or to fit things like this set of letters to a metal surface. Magnets can be made of any strength. It is therefore important to choose the strength suitable for the task.

Make a magnet
Some materials can be made into magnets. They are made of iron or steel. Not all steels can be made into magnets, however, because they have been mixed with other materials. Stainless steel, for example, cannot be made into a magnet.

To make a magnet you need a magnet and an iron or steel rod like a screwdriver.

Move the magnet along the iron rod, stroking it from one end to the other. When you get to the far end lift the magnet away and take it back to the start before stroking again. After a few strokes you will have a new magnetised screwdriver.

Try out your screwdriver magnet and see what it will pick up. You will find that it is much easier to hold a screw once the screwdriver has been magnetised.

This piece of rock is called a loadstone. It is made of a special form of iron. Its magnetic powers are shown by the way it holds all the tiny iron filings on its surface

Follow the field

Magnets produce an invisible force which you can find using a compass or tiny pieces of iron called iron filings.

Because iron filings are small, they make patterns that show you what is really going on.

Iron filings help you to find the invisible forces of a magnet and even make magnetic mountains.

Why a compass works
The Earth acts as a giant bar magnet. This is because the centre of the Earth contains a lot of molten iron that is continually moving.

Compasses have been used for navigation for centuries. A compass is a small needle of magnetic metal that is attracted by the magnetic north or south poles of the Earth.

You can make a compass by stroking a needle with a magnet. Put it on a piece of packing foam and float it on saucer of water. The needle will automatically line up with the Earth's magnetic field.

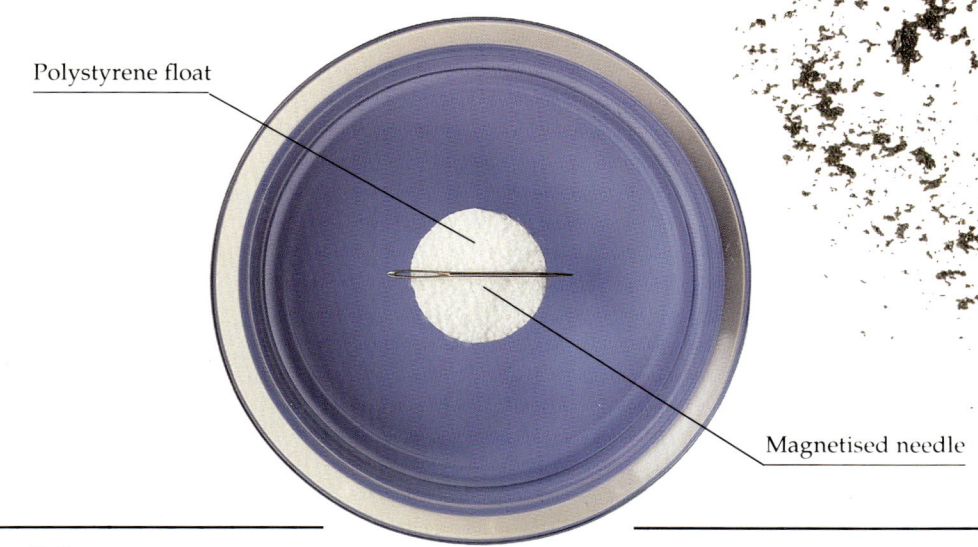

Polystyrene float

Magnetised needle

Filings fields
Filings can be made to move about. Start with filings spread evenly on a sheet of cardboard.

Hold the cardboard up and move a magnet about *under* the cardboard.

Because the magnet's force goes through the cardboard the filings will move as if by magic.

This is the kind of magnet used to make the pattern

Follow the filings
You can buy filings or you can make them yourself by filing a rod of iron or mild steel.

Spread out some filings on a sheet of paper. Now place a bar magnet *on* the middle of the paper and see what happens. The magnet will get a fur coat.

Look at the pattern of the filings. Their shape shows you the pattern of the magnetic field.

Metal detector
You can look for iron pipes, nails and girders that may be hidden inside walls using a compass. A compass needle will swing slightly when it comes near to an iron or steel object.

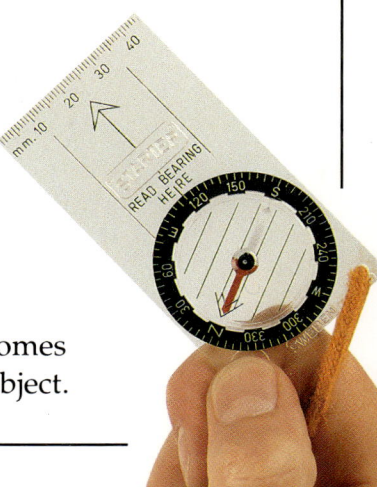

Magnets on demand

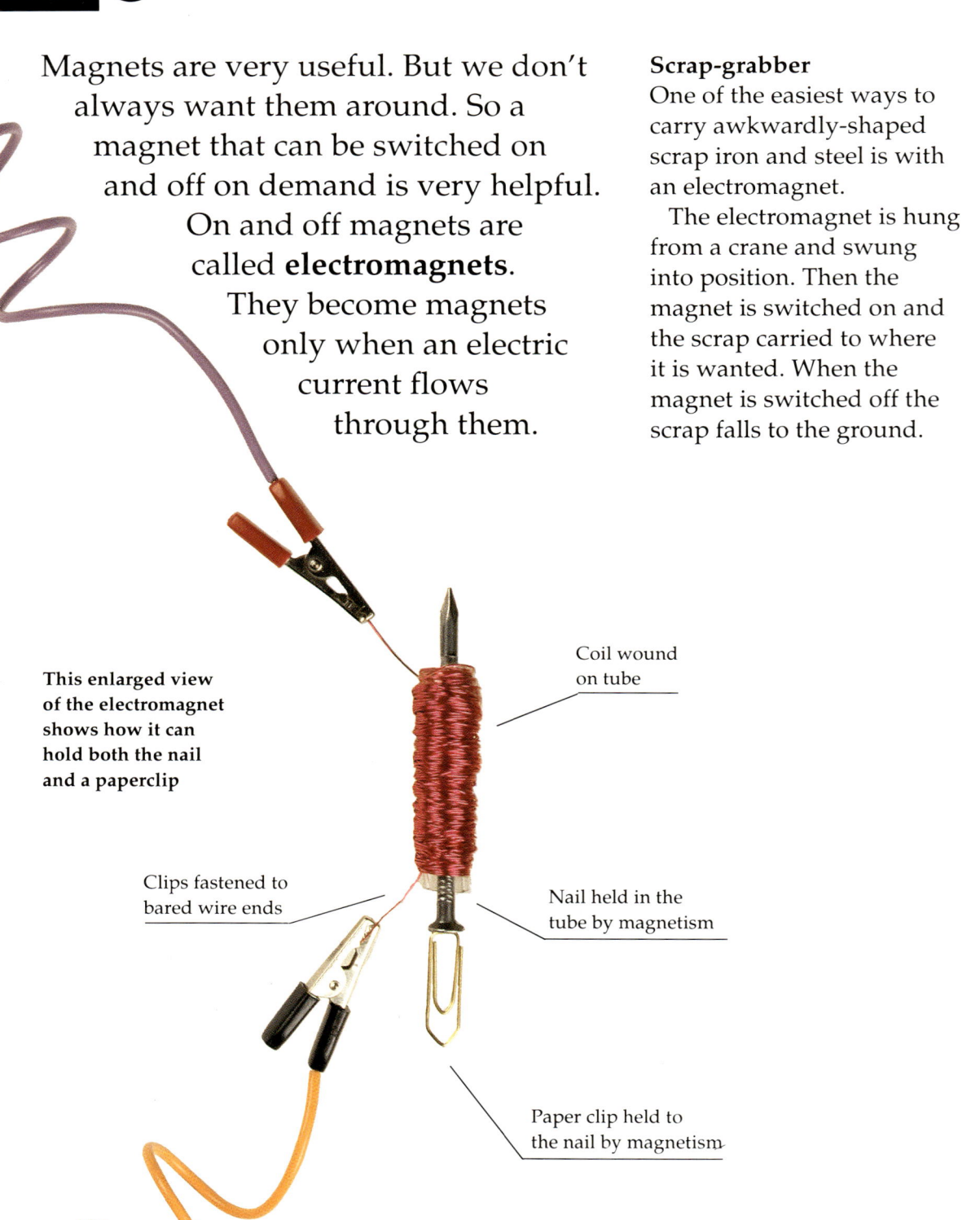

Magnets are very useful. But we don't always want them around. So a magnet that can be switched on and off on demand is very helpful. On and off magnets are called **electromagnets**. They become magnets only when an electric current flows through them.

Scrap-grabber
One of the easiest ways to carry awkwardly-shaped scrap iron and steel is with an electromagnet.

The electromagnet is hung from a crane and swung into position. Then the magnet is switched on and the scrap carried to where it is wanted. When the magnet is switched off the scrap falls to the ground.

This enlarged view of the electromagnet shows how it can hold both the nail and a paperclip

Coil wound on tube

Clips fastened to bared wire ends

Nail held in the tube by magnetism

Paper clip held to the nail by magnetism

Compass

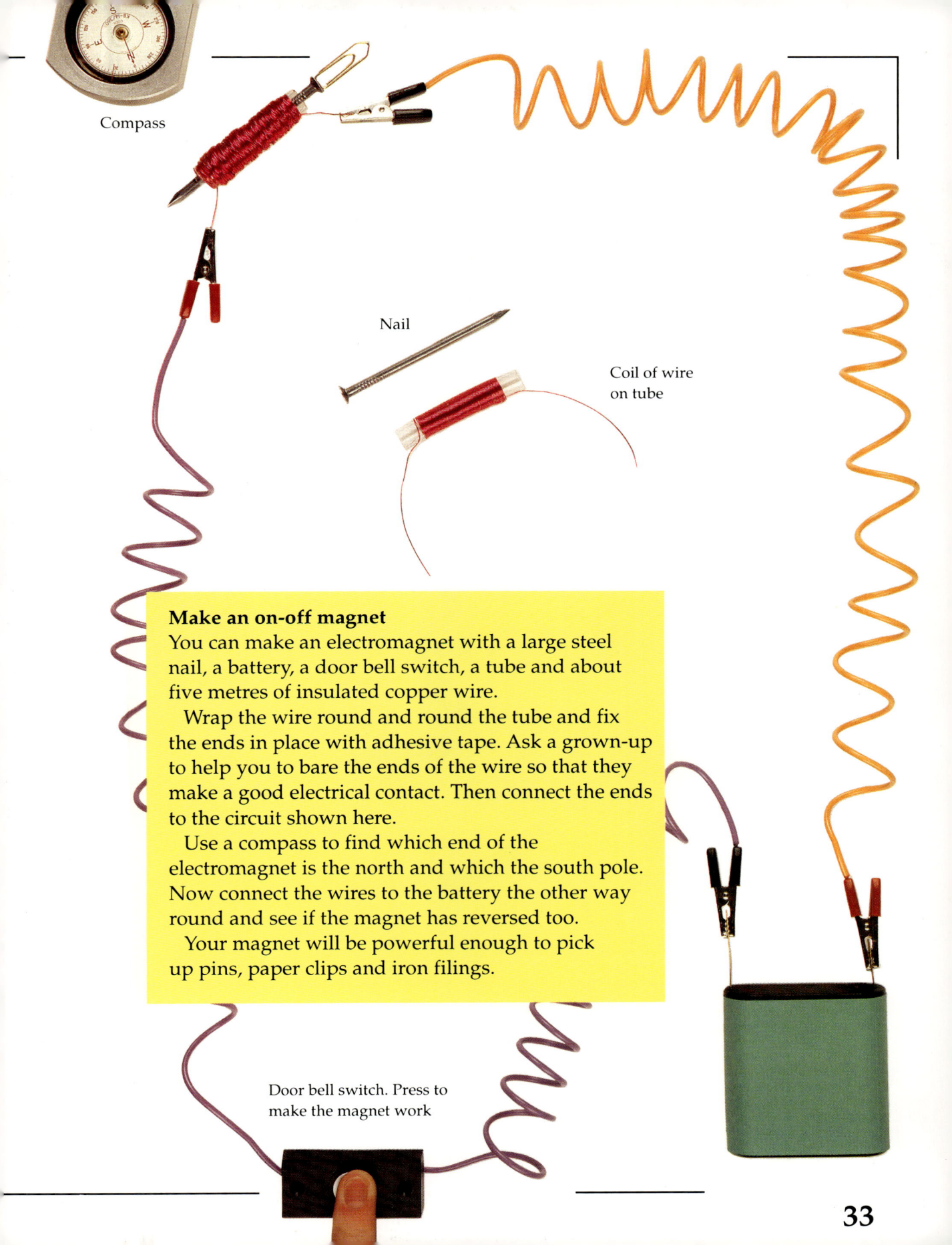

Nail

Coil of wire on tube

Make an on-off magnet

You can make an electromagnet with a large steel nail, a battery, a door bell switch, a tube and about five metres of insulated copper wire.

Wrap the wire round and round the tube and fix the ends in place with adhesive tape. Ask a grown-up to help you to bare the ends of the wire so that they make a good electrical contact. Then connect the ends to the circuit shown here.

Use a compass to find which end of the electromagnet is the north and which the south pole. Now connect the wires to the battery the other way round and see if the magnet has reversed too.

Your magnet will be powerful enough to pick up pins, paper clips and iron filings.

Door bell switch. Press to make the magnet work

Magnets with a memory

It's surprising how much we use magnets. One of the most common places is in a cassette recorder, another is a computer. By using magnets we can store enormous amounts of information accurately.

Two way message

Magnets don't have to look like bars. Some of the most useful are shaped into tapes and discs.

A cassette tape is a long plastic ribbon coated with minute iron particles (look for the non-shiny side).

As the tape moves it goes past a tiny electromagnet called a recording head. Electric signals reaching the recording head set up patterns of magnetism on the tape.

When the tape is played back the tape's magnetism 'fingerprint' causes electric signals in the playback head. These are then made larger using the cassette player's electronics and are finally played through a loudspeaker or earphones.

This is a video-tape used to record and playback sound and pictures on to a TV screen. It is much wider than an audio, or sound, tape because information about pictures as well as sound has to be stored

Cleaning up

You can prove that cassette tapes contain magnetic information. Get an *old* tape that you don't want any more. Rub a strong bar magnet along part of the tape and play this section of tape. The funny sound you hear will be the effect of the magnet. It has affected the magnetic fingerprint, causing a loss of information.

Computer disks

Computers store information on disks that look something like a record. The disk – often called floppy disk because it is made of bendy plastic – has an iron coating on its surface.

The computer 'reads' from and 'writes' on to the disk using a small head just like the tape recorder. The disk shown here has 800 000 different pieces of information stored on it in magnetic form. The biggest disks can store many millions of pieces of information.

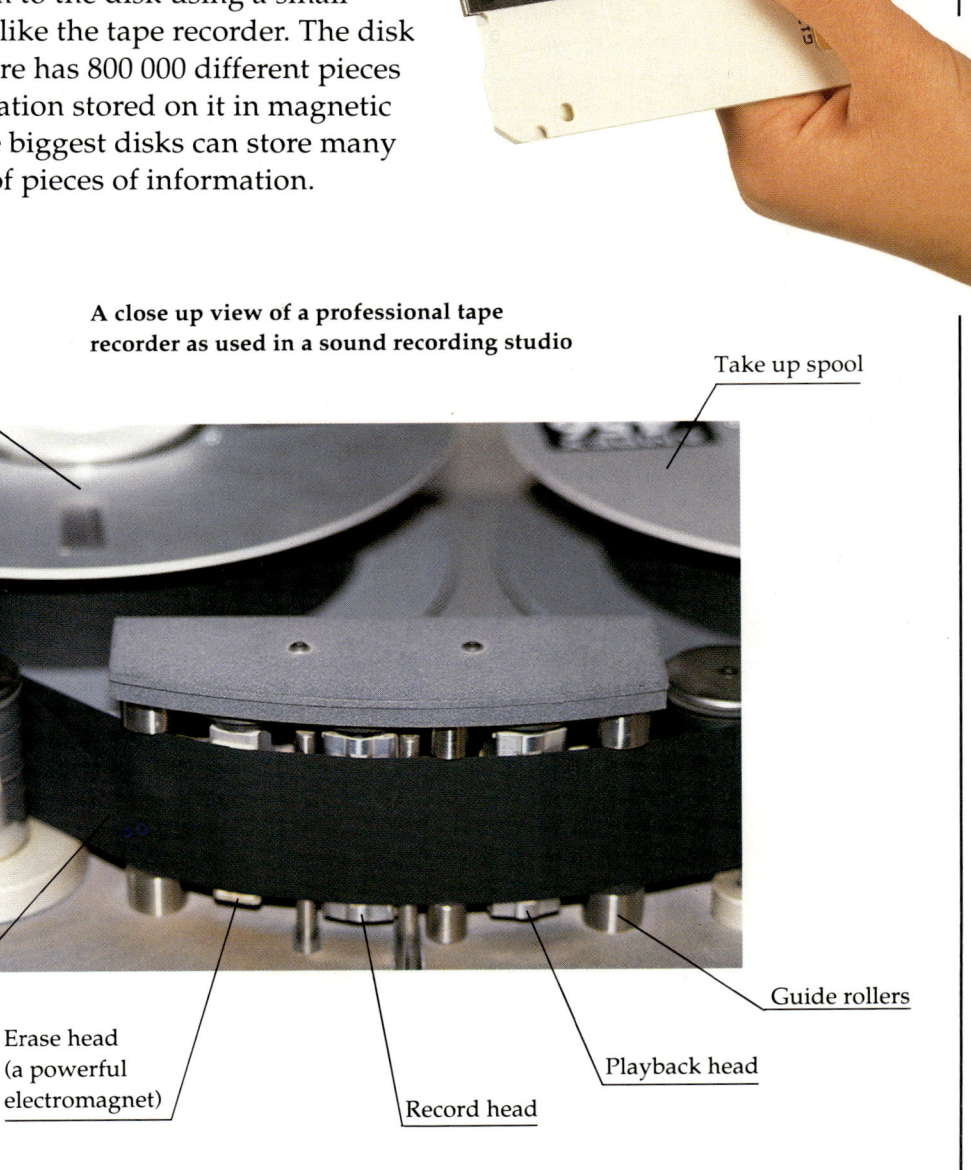

A close up view of a professional tape recorder as used in a sound recording studio

- Supply spool
- Take up spool
- Magnetic tape
- Erase head (a powerful electromagnet)
- Record head
- Playback head
- Guide rollers

Electric motor

Electric motors show that electricity and magnetism cannot be separated. When a magnet is moved across a coil of wire it makes an electric current flow in the wire. This is how electricity is made in power stations.

When electricity flows through a coil of wire, it can make a magnet and spin a shaft. This is how a motor works. Motors and generators are just the reverse of each other.

This electric train is powered by electric motors. This gives a quiet, clean means of transport

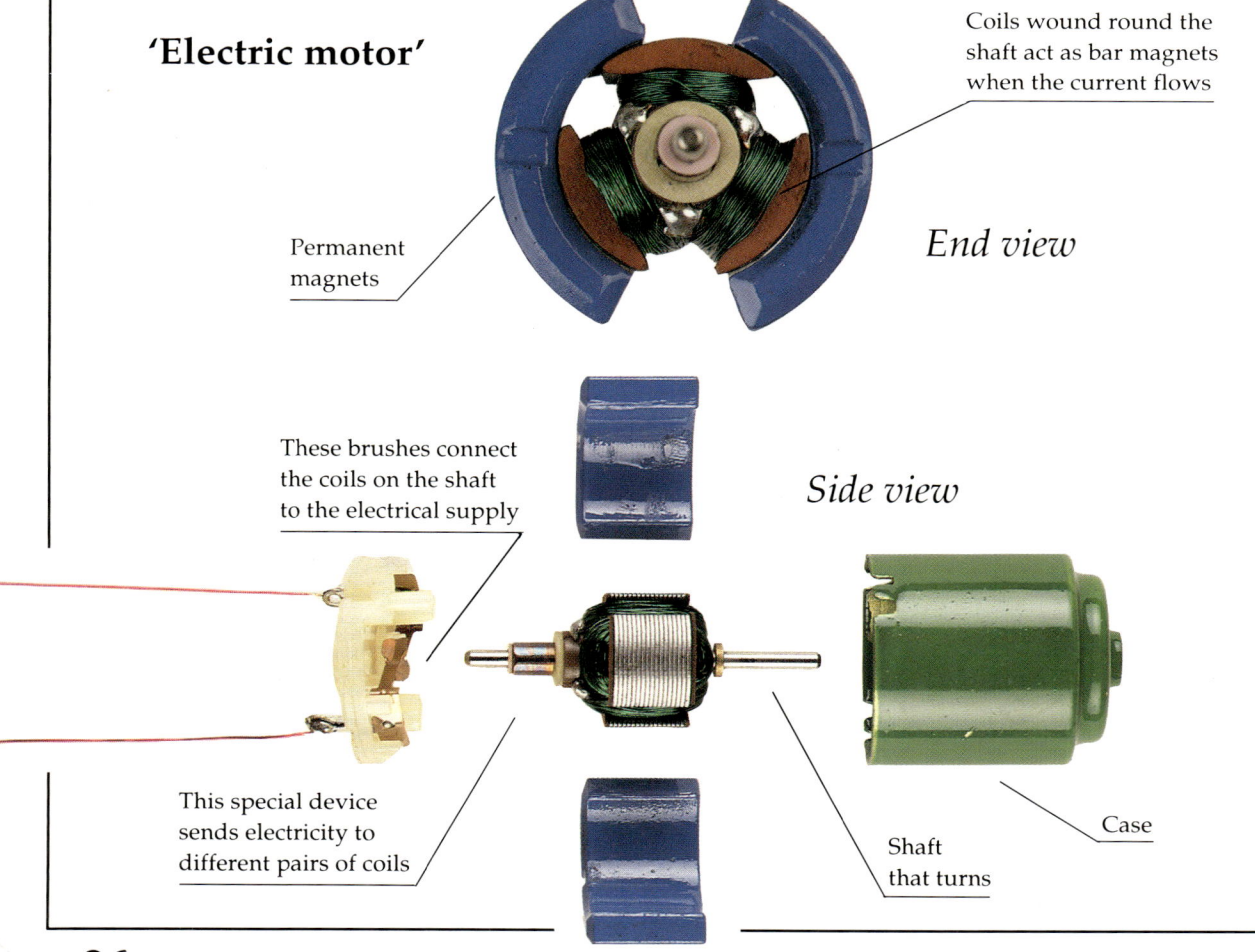

'Electric motor'

Permanent magnets

Coils wound round the shaft act as bar magnets when the current flows

End view

These brushes connect the coils on the shaft to the electrical supply

Side view

This special device sends electricity to different pairs of coils

Shaft that turns

Case

Copper wire

Arm

Baseboard

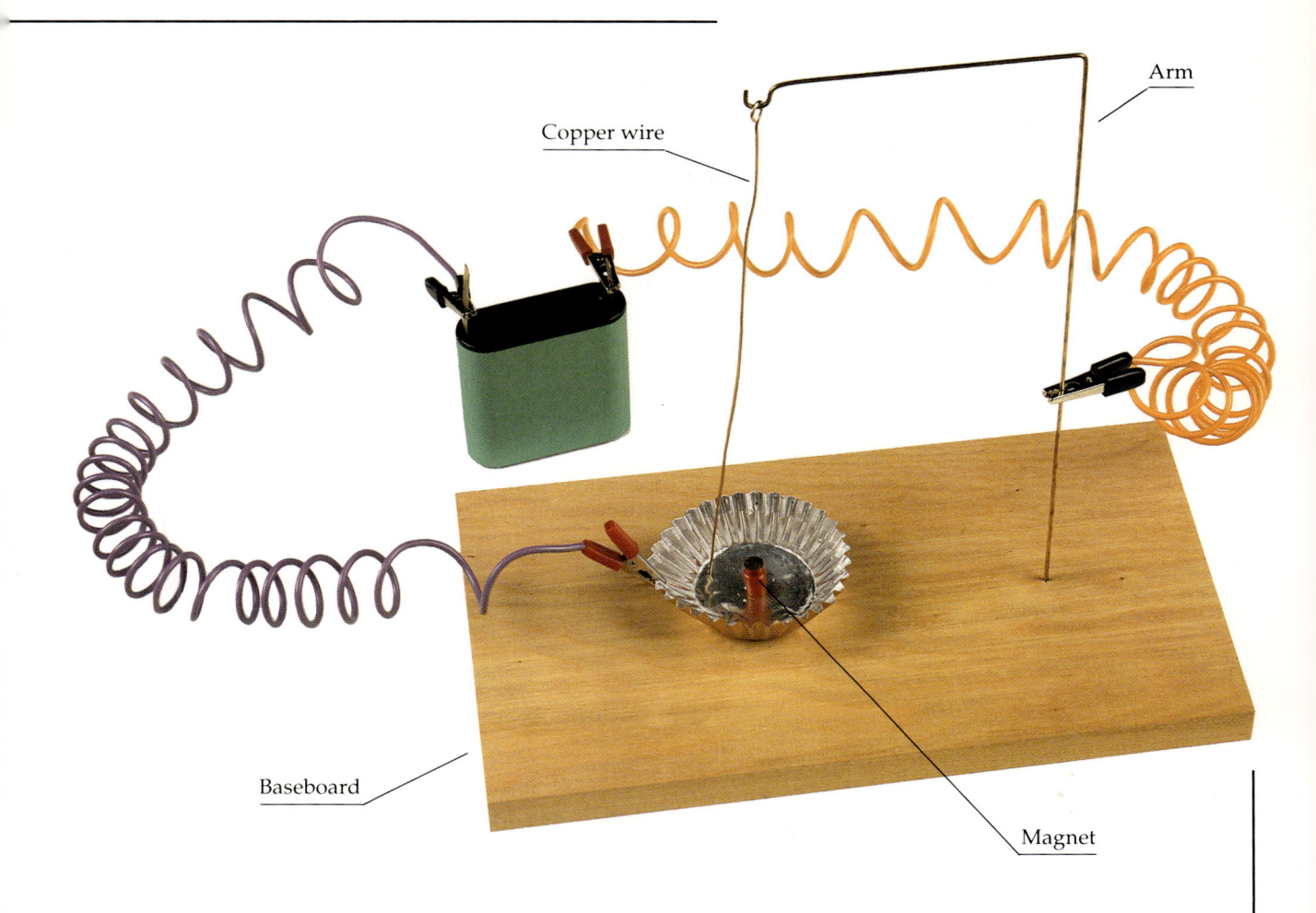

Magnet

Make your own motor

This is a version of the first electric motor. It was made 170 years ago by Michael Faraday, the scientist most responsible for discovering the way electricity works.

You will need to ask a grown-up to help with this. Start with a small metal cake case. Make up as strong a solution of salty water as you can. Keep adding salt until no more will dissolve. Pour the solution into the case. Place a small barrel magnet in the middle.

You next need to suspend a stiff copper wire over the case. Use a long piece of stiff wire and bend it into an arm like the one in the picture. Push it into a hole drilled in the baseboard. Make a hook at one end and then fit another wire long enough to dangle in the salt water.

Using crocodile clips, connect a battery to the cake case and to the copper arm.

The motor should start up immediately.

How Faraday's motor works

The electricity flows through the wire and the salty water. This sets up a magnetic field around the wire and the wire is then pushed away by the barrel magnet.

The wire goes round and round the magnet, trying to fall back to rest but while the current flows it never can.

Tell the world

Sending electrical signals along a wire changed the world. It allowed people separated by long distances to send and receive messages almost instantly. The device that did it was called a telegraph.

Operator sending a message on a Morse printing telegraph about 1887. Notice the sending switch by the operator's right hand. The battery is under the table

Make a telegraph
The telegraph circuit is very simple. It consists of a battery, a switch and a buzzer or bulb. Connect it up as shown here. To make a long distance telegraph connect the buzzer to the battery and the door bell switch using 'bell wire'. Any shop that sells buzzers will have the wire.

The door bell switch and the battery make up a 'transmitter'. The buzzer or bulb is a receiver. The distance between transmitter and receiver can be as long as you wish. Now use the Morse code shown on the page opposite to send a signal.

Door bell switch

Bulb

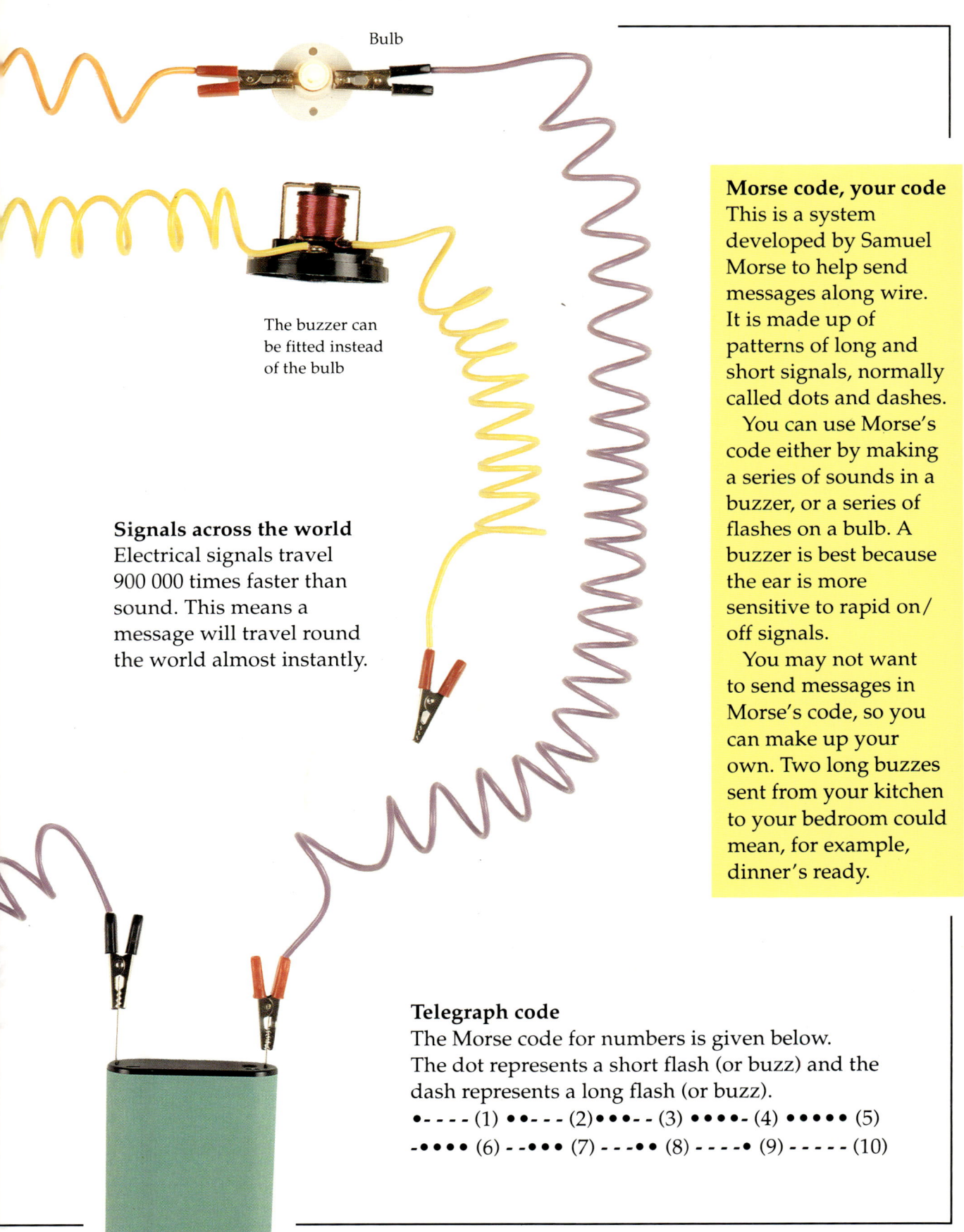

The buzzer can be fitted instead of the bulb

Signals across the world
Electrical signals travel 900 000 times faster than sound. This means a message will travel round the world almost instantly.

Morse code, your code
This is a system developed by Samuel Morse to help send messages along wire. It is made up of patterns of long and short signals, normally called dots and dashes.

You can use Morse's code either by making a series of sounds in a buzzer, or a series of flashes on a bulb. A buzzer is best because the ear is more sensitive to rapid on/off signals.

You may not want to send messages in Morse's code, so you can make up your own. Two long buzzes sent from your kitchen to your bedroom could mean, for example, dinner's ready.

Telegraph code
The Morse code for numbers is given below. The dot represents a short flash (or buzz) and the dash represents a long flash (or buzz).
• - - - - (1) • • - - - (2) • • • - - (3) • • • • - (4) • • • • • (5)
- • • • • (6) - - • • • (7) - - - • • (8) - - - - • (9) - - - - - (10)

39

The speaking magnet

The telephone was developed to make long distance speech possible without the use of Morse code. It lets us talk to people all over the world using on–off magnets.

The first telephone
Alexander Graham Bell, a Scotsman who had emigrated to America, used the principle of magnetism to send electricity down a wire.

He put a very thin disc of iron near to a coil of wire. The coil had a barrel magnet inside. When somebody spoke the sound waves pushed against the iron disc and made it move. As the disc moved, so it made electricity flow in the coil.

Bell used two of these instruments joined together with a battery.

Receiver. Electrical signals cause an electromagnet to vibrate a disc and make sound waves

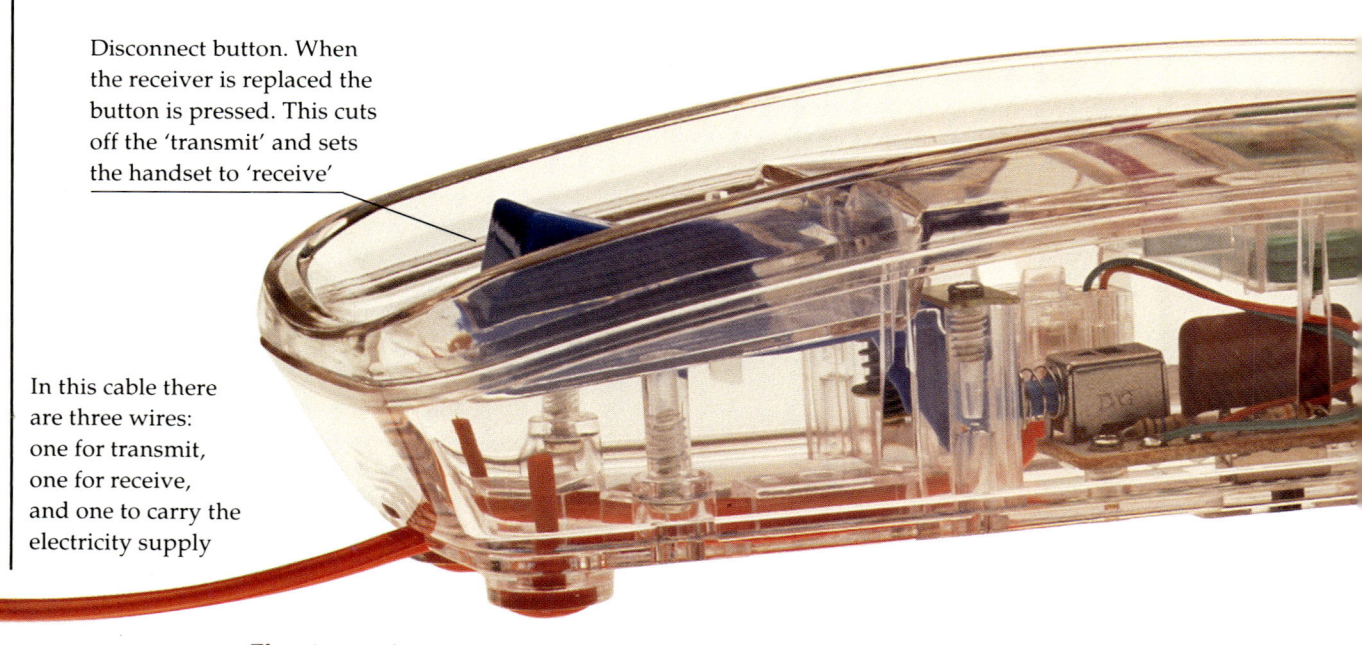

Disconnect button. When the receiver is replaced the button is pressed. This cuts off the 'transmit' and sets the handset to 'receive'

In this cable there are three wires: one for transmit, one for receive, and one to carry the electricity supply

Electric signals flow along the wire

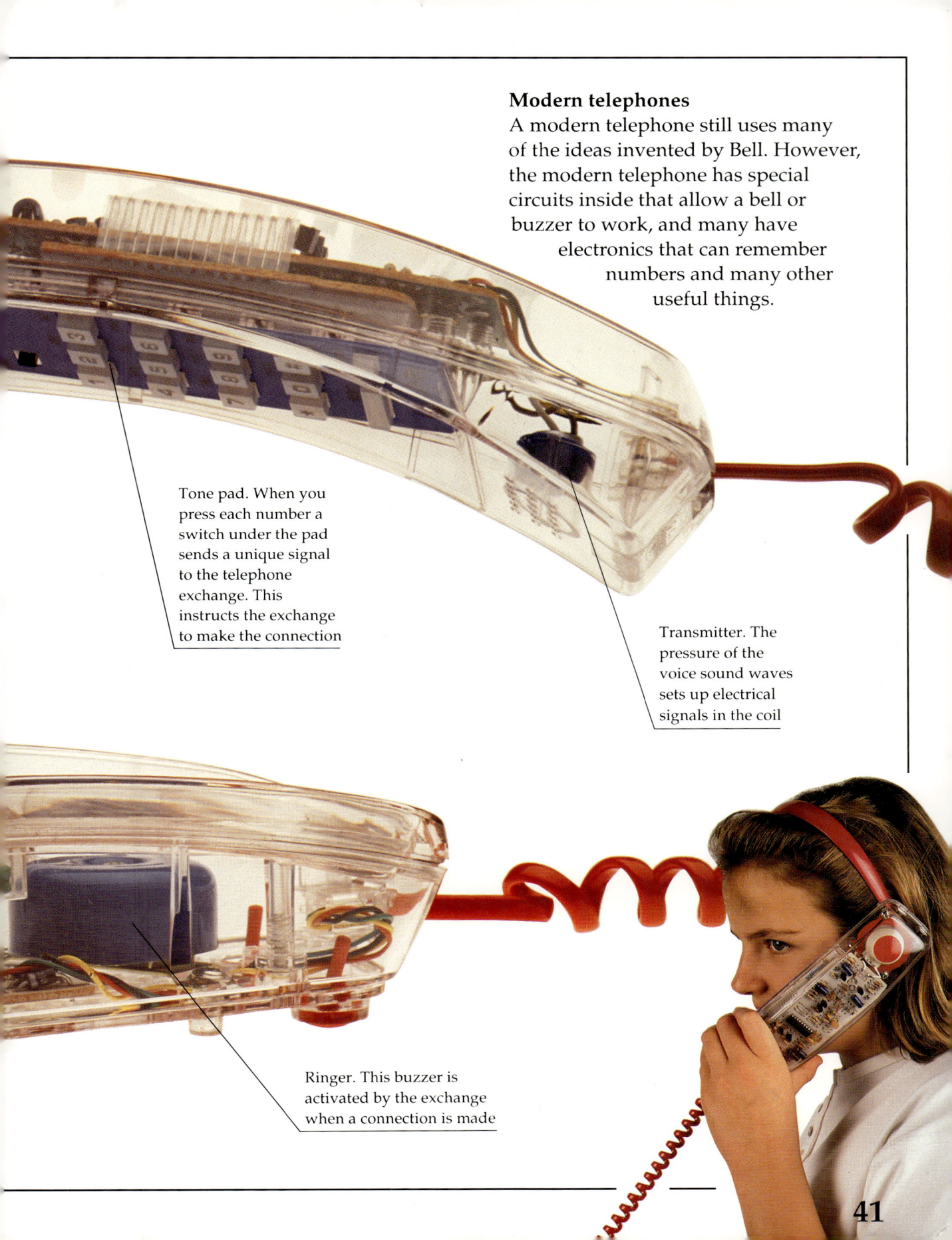

Modern telephones
A modern telephone still uses many of the ideas invented by Bell. However, the modern telephone has special circuits inside that allow a bell or buzzer to work, and many have electronics that can remember numbers and many other useful things.

Tone pad. When you press each number a switch under the pad sends a unique signal to the telephone exchange. This instructs the exchange to make the connection

Transmitter. The pressure of the voice sound waves sets up electrical signals in the coil

Ringer. This buzzer is activated by the exchange when a connection is made

Making electricity

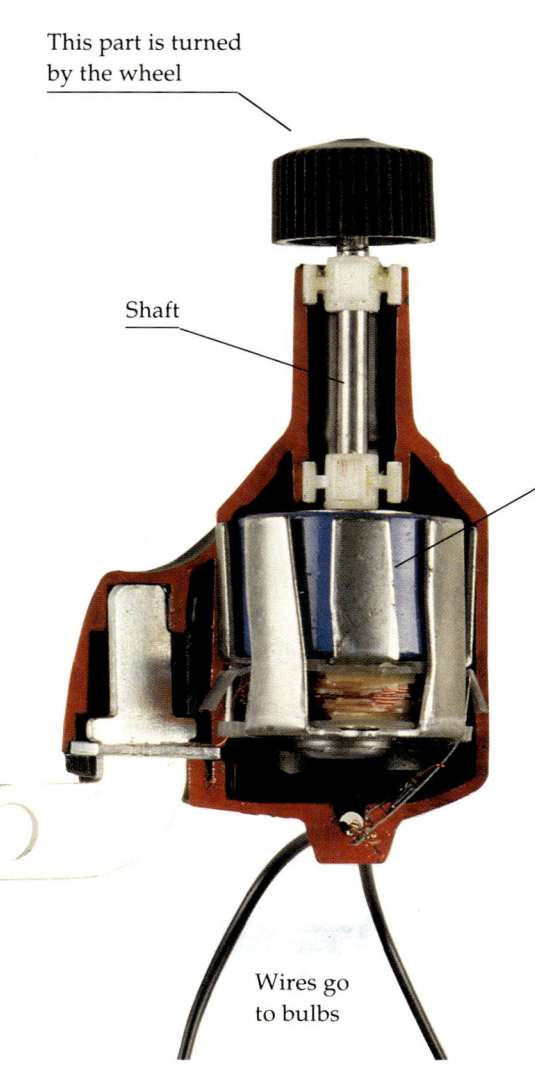

Electricity is an essential part of our world. The places where it is made are called power stations, and they are connected to our homes and factories by networks of cables called a power **grid**.

This part is turned by the wheel

Shaft

As the shaft turns, it moves a coil inside the magnets and electricity is produced. This lights the bicycle bulbs

Find out about generating
Ask a grown-up to help you to turn a bike upside down so it rests on its handlebars.
 Ask them to hold the frame firmly while you attach the dynamo and peddle using your hands.
 The brightness of the headlight and tail-light bulbs is a measure of the amount of electricity you are generating. Notice how the amount of electricity changes as you peddle fast or slow.
 In this case you are converting the chemical energy of your food into power for your muscles and using this to make electricity. It is not a very efficient system.

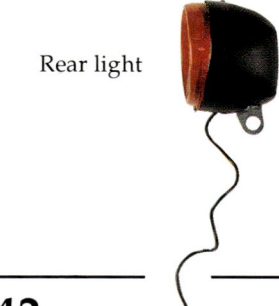

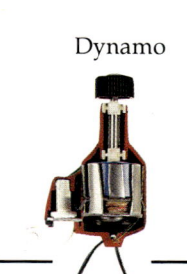

Wires go to bulbs

Rear light

Dynamo

Front light

Power stations

A power station is like a large version of the bike dynamo. Often there will be several dynamos – or generators – running together.

The generator shafts are usually turned by steam. In turn the steam is made by boiling water using coal, oil or gas. The electricity is then fed into the power grid.

Renewable energy

Power stations are expensive to run and they use huge amounts of fuel. Burning the fuel sends enormous amounts of gases into the air which may produce **acid rain** and may partly cause the **greenhouse effect**.

There are some alternative ways of generating electricity that do not cause air pollution. The waves, the wind and the Sun can each provide more electricity than we need, but at the moment nobody has been able to invent ways of converting these sources on a large scale.

Some generators are turned by flowing water. These **hydroelectric** power stations are placed beside reservoirs or fast flowing rivers. The flowing water is used to turn a kind of paddle wheel called a turbine which is connected to a generator.

A power station provides high voltage electrical pressure which is fed along cables suspended from pylons. The current flowing has to be sufficient for all the homes to which it is connected

This collection of wind turbines is called a wind farm. Each propeller is connected to a dynamo. This wind farm is in California, USA

43

Magnets in space

Electricity and magnetism are common in the sky. Electricity makes the thunder and lightning that comes with a big storm. Magnetism makes the great night-time glow that is seen near the poles.

The power from each of these common natural effects is greater than the all the power we could ever make on Earth.

Night-time lights
The autumn and spring nights near the Poles are often the scene of amazing coloured flares in the sky. These flares are called auroras and they look like huge curtain fireworks.

The auroras are caused by the Earth's magnetic field, which catches some of the invisible gases released by the Sun (called the Solar Wind) and turns them into electric flares. The effect is rather like when you switch on a fluorescent lighting tube. But this lighting tube is thousands of kilometres long.

A camper watches the night-time sky. The bottom of this **luminous** curtain is about 100 kilometres above the ground, while the top is over 300 kilometres high. Notice how it appears to fold into pleats just like a real curtain.

New words

acid rain
when fossil fuels such as coal, oil and gas are burned in power stations and in car engines large amounts of a gas called sulphur dioxide are produced. This gas drifts up into the air and mixes with water droplets in the clouds. The raindrops that fall are acid. Acid rain can kill trees and the fish in lakes

appliance
the name given to any electrical equipment used in the home, for example a washing machine or a stove. It could also mean a radio or TV

charge
the amount of stored electrical energy present. People often speak of 'charging a battery'. What they mean is that they must replace the electrical energy that has been used. To do this they use a piece of equipment called a 'charger'

circuit
any collection of electrical components that are connected in such a way that electricity flows. Radios, TVs and computers have very complicated circuits with thousands of connections

dimmer
a piece of electrical equipment that cuts down the voltage that reaches a light bulb. With less voltage (pressure) the bulb then glows less brightly and uses less electric current

electrical energy
the electrical power that is available to make appliances work

electromagnet
a form of temporary magnetism produced whenever an electric current flows in a wire. Temporary magnetism is very useful for operating switches by remote control

filament
the fine wire that is used in light bulbs. The wire is made of a special metal that will not easily melt even when it becomes white hot. Because the metal would burn away in air, a filament is placed in a glass bulb with a gas called argon

greenhouse effect
when fossil fuels such as coal, oil and gas are burned they release a gas called carbon dioxide. This gas occurs naturally in the air, but the amount has doubled this century due to fuel burning. Carbon dioxide traps heat and makes the atmosphere warmer. The way it works is often said to be similar to the way a greenhouse warms up, so people call it the greenhouse effect

grid
a network of cables that allow power stations to be linked to homes. A grid allows electricity to be shared, so the power can be sent to wherever it is needed. The tall pylons crossing the countryside carry cables that are part of the power grid

hydroelectric
a term meaning water-driven. Hydroelectric power is obtained by damming water in a reservoir and then releasing it in a tunnel. Inside the tunnel is a wheel called a turbine, that is turned by the rushing water. The wheel turns the shaft of a generator which in turn makes electricity

luminous
a material that glows when certain types of light shine on it, or which gives out light because of the way magnetism affects it

overloaded
a term meaning that more electrical current is flowing than the system can handle. At home an overloaded system will cause a fuse to blow

parallel
when electrical items such as bulbs are connected in parallel, each item is directly connected to the supply. The current flows from the negative terminal to the positive terminal through each item at the same time

pole
the name given to each end of a line. The Earth acts like a long magnet with its ends, or poles, near to the North Pole and the South Pole. As a result the magnetic poles are also called north and south. North and south poles are also used to describe the ends of all other magnets

power
the rate at which electrical energy is fed into or taken out of a circuit. It is usually measured in watts

solar
a name give to the Sun. Solar energy is the light energy of the Sun. Plants use this energy to make their tissues. Scientists expect solar energy to become very important as a means of power for people in the next century

static
a form of electric charge that builds up on the surface of some objects. If the charge gets big enough a spark can jump the gap. Lightning is caused this way

Index

acid rain 43, 46
air 13
appliance 6, 14, 17, 20, 46
aurora 44

balloons 8
battery 6, 24
Bell 40

cables 6, 12, 14
calculator 25
carbon 24
cassettes 34
charge 8, 11, 46
circuit 7, 33, 46
comb 9
compass 30
conductor 12
copper 24
current 6, 32

dimmer 16, 46
dry battery 25
dynamo 42

Earth's magnetism 30, 44
electric motor 36
electroplating 26
electrode 10
electromagnets 32, 46
energy 6, 22, 46
erasing 35

Faraday 37
field pattern 31
filament 16, 46
fluorescent tubes 22
fuse 17

generator 36, 42
greenhouse effect 43, 46
grid 42, 47

hair 9
handset 40
heating 16
home supply 14
horse-shoe magnet 29
hydroelectric power 43, 47

insulator 12
iron 29
iron filings 28, 31

kettle 22

Las Vegas, USA 23
lemon battery 24
lighting 11, 16
lightning conductor 11
loadstone 28
luminous 45, 47

magnet 28
magnetic catches 28
magnetic field 30
magnetic tape 34
magnetism 28
mains 20
making magnets 29
meter 15, 23
Morse code 39

nature 10
negative charge 7
nerves 10

overloaded 17, 47

pacemaker 10
parallel circuit 20, 21, 47
party lights 19
playback head 34
poles 28, 30, 47
positive charge 7
power 14, 47
power grid 42
power station 7, 43
pylons 7, 12

receiver 39, 40
rechargeable batteries 25
recording 35

saving energy 22
scrap-grabber 32
series circuit 18
shock 10
solar panel 24, 25, 47
Solar Wind 44
spark 8
static 8, 47

telegraph 38
telephone 40
thunder 11
transmitter 39

Van de Graaff 9
voltage 6

watt 22
wind generator 43